With longing to my beloved mother, Tema Blum

HANDMADE CHOCOLATE
Adi Endevelt

www.adi-candies.co.il

Editing: Shlomit Perry | "Word for Word"
Translated and Edited: Dana Smadja
Photographs: Shai Afgin
Book & Cover Design: Miri Nistor | Dodo Design

© 2016, Hebrew edition
© 2018, English edition

handmade.fudgecandy@gmail.com

All rights of the book, its contents and photographs are reserved for Adi Endevelt. No copying, duplicating, photographing, translating, recording, presenting, storing in a database or distributing of this book or part of it is permitted in any way, whether electronically, optically, mechanically, or otherwise. Any commercial or non-commercial use of this book (or any part of it) requires a permit from the owner of the rights.

Instructional videos of select recipes may also be found on the YouTube channel "Adi Endevelt".

— ADI ENDEVELT —

CONTENTS

How it all Began   6
About the Book   8
Getting to work   10
   Special Equipment   10
   Ingredients   10
   Tempering the Chocolate   11

SIMPLE CHOCOLATE CANDIES

Warm Chocolatey Drink   14
Peanut Butter Candy   15
Chocolate Sandwich Spread   16
Soft Chocolate Candy   18
Chocolate Tahini Candies   20
Chocolate Fudge   21
Easy Chocolate Fudge   22
Chocolate Coconut Candy   23
Chocolate Popcorn   24
Crunchy Chocolate with Almonds   26
Chocolate Disks   27
Cornflakes Candy   28
Chocolate Lollipop   30
Chocolate Nut Layers   31
Chocolate & Seed Candy   32

TRUFFLES

Chocolate Truffles – Basic Recipe   36
Truffles with Alcohol   38
Coconut Truffles   40
Nut Truffles   41
Fruit Truffles   42

CHOCOLATE CANDIES WITH FILLING

Homemade chocolate cups   46
Basic Chocolate Ganache   47
White Chocolate Ganache & Fruit Filling   48
Hazelnut or Pistachio Filling   49
Cheese Filling   50
Pina Colada Filling   51
Marshmallow Cream Filling   52
Toffee Filling   54

HOW IT ALL BEGAN

During a family trip to Northern England in 2000, we came across a small boutique candy factory in one of the villages and we were watching the preparation of lemon-flavored candies.

The sweet aroma of sugar syrup, cooked in a large copper pot, tempted me to stay there drawn to a caramel flavored candy bar, which had a mixture of airy and crunchy textures. I asked the confectioner what this candy was made of, and he was only willing to tell me one word: sugar.

My curiosity led me to search for recipes for candies in bookstores around England, but it turned out that the recipes were omitted from cookbooks during the first half of the 20th century since the candies became industrialized and therefore much cheaper and more available, and so there was no longer a reason to prepare them at home.

The idea of candy making excited me, and so whenever I went abroad I was searching for recipes in old cookbooks – at thrift stores and in libraries. Three years later, while I was browsing through a small booklet of recipes for candies, I found the recipe for that crunchy candy I tasted in England back then. With great enthusiasm I went to prepare it, but the result was not successful. So I threw it away and tried again and again... until...I finally succeeded. Soon thereafter, I began to attempt to prepare more candies. Very soon I realized that this process is actually an exact science and therefore I read professional articles about the chemistry of sugar in general, and about confectionery in particular. As soon as I was able to make a selection of candy with which I was satisfied, I knew that this is what I wanted to pursue from then on in a professional manner, at which point I established my own brand, "Handmade Candies".

I traveled to England many times thereafter to be trained, observe and learn from confectioners of hand crafted candies, to acquire tips and sometimes even recipes. In addition to the making of candies and inventing new recipes, I researched the history of candy making, which I found very fascinating; information that I share in my own workshops. Each candy we prepare in the workshops has a special interesting story of its own.

Chocolate is one of many candies in which many other candies may be combined. After more than a decade working with candies, I decided to attend a long chocolatier course in order to enrich my knowledge and the variety of candies that I prepare.

For over a decade I have been creating recipes for candies, inventing new ones and changing existing ones. I prepare all of them using the traditional methods, as have been prepared in home kitchens 100 and more years ago. This way, the candies created have a special and high quality texture and a unique surprising taste.

ABOUT THE BOOK

Chocolate is one of the candies for which an entire book can be dedicated. It can be found in cakes, mousses, creams, spreads, puddings, beverages, liqueurs, ice cream, marinades for meats, and of course in chocolate-based candies or as a candy coating.

So I dedicate this book to chocolate.

Who doesn't love chocolate? This is a candy made of cacao, sugar, lecithin, and sometimes milk. Beyond just its amazing flavor, most chocolate candies have the perfect texture and melt in your mouth. When eating chocolate, it has a creamy deliciousness, and always serves as the perfect treat.

There are those who like their chocolate sweet and milky, and those who prefer it very bitter. There are those who prefer their chocolate crunchy, with the addition of various chopped nuts and almonds or even with the addition of sea salt, and there are those who enjoy their chocolate with dried fruit. Of course there are those that enjoy their chocolate as is, with no additions, and those who enjoy their chocolates filled with various fruit or liqueur fillings.

What all these people have in common, is that they all love the intoxicating and wonderful flavor of chocolate.

I will be the first to admit that I oftentimes feel like eating chocolate...even a lot of it....and after I eat chocolate, I feel good, euphoric, and satisfied.

Chocolate is a household item – found in most pantries, given as gifts to loved ones, to express appreciation, and served when hosting. You too can prepare chocolate candies at home – there is no need to be a chocolatier or take a course in order to prepare spectacular chocolate candies yourself.

In this booklet, you will find recipes, most of which are easy to prepare, that may be prepared in your home kitchen, and served to your family, friends and guests, or to give as a gift – sharing your handmade delicacies.

I hope that when you prepare these chocolate candies, you will see how easy they are to make, and continue to make more and more of them!

The beauty in these recipes is that you can always add your own variations to each recipe, varying fillings and flavors as you wish.

There are certain chocolate candies where tempering the chocolate is recommended, and those where tempering is unnecessary. For methods of tempering, please refer to page 11.

(tempering = reaching a certain temperature and then reducing the temperature in order to create a shiny hard chocolate that melts in your mouth).

GETTING TO WORK

SPECIAL EQUIPMENT

Measuring Cups and Spoons
When the recipe indicates the measurement of one cup or one spoon it refers to a flat cup or a flat spoon, accordingly.

Thermometer
It may be either an analog or a digital thermometer.

Candy Sticks
Plastic and paper sticks are sold in specialty stores.

Molds
These come in various cavity shapes. The cavities should be small since sweets taste much better and delicious when presented in these size.

INGREDIENTS

Chocolate
Raw chocolate may be found in the market in the form of different sized coins or in chunks, which have to be chopped before use. The higher the percentage of cacao in the chocolate, the bitterer and better quality the chocolate.

Concentrated Fruit Puree
This is an excellent alternative to food coloring and flavor extracts, as it combines flavor and color. It may be purchased in specialty cooking stores.

Food Coloring
There are natural and artificial colorings. Begin with a very small amount, even just one drop and add more gradually if necessary.

Flavor Extract
There are natural and artificial flavor extracts. The more concentrated the extract, the smaller amount required.

Nuts
Any kind of nuts may be used, as desired, unless specified in a particular recipe.

Pistachio and Nut Puree, bresilienne, Small Chocolate Cups
These may be purchased in specialty stores.

TEMPERING THE CHOCOLATE

Melt the raw chocolate either in a double boiler (make sure that the bowl in the pot will not touch the water, but that it will be the steam in contact with the pot that will melt the chocolate) or by melting the chocolate in the microwave by heating it for thirty seconds and stirring and repeating until the chocolate has completely melted. The chocolate should reach approx. 40°C (104°F) and then may be cooled in one of three ways:

1. Add 2-3 coins of chocolate to the melted chocolate and stir until fully melted. Repeat this process until the coins will no longer melt and continue to stir until the chocolate reaches 32°C (89.6°F).

2. Melt ⅔ of the amount of chocolate that the recipe calls for, then add the remaining ⅓ of the chocolate to the melted chocolate, stirring until all is melted. Continue to stir until the chocolate reaches a temperature of 32°C (89.6°F).

3. On a cold marble surface, pour the melted chocolate and using a metal spatula, move the chocolate from side to side in a rotational manner until cool.

After the chocolate has been tempered proceed according to the recipe.

{ 1 }

SIMPLE CHOCOLATE CANDIES

In this chapter you will find chocolate recipes that are easy to prepare.

This chapter will introduce chocolate candies for

both kids and adults for various occasions.

Some of the candies are rich with additions and others are almost entirely chocolate.

Rest assured, despite their ease of preparation, every recipe is absolutely delicious!

WARM CHOCOLATEY DRINK

Ingredients for 2 servings:

2 flat teaspoons of cacao powder

2 tablespoons of sugar

¼ cup of hot water

2 cups of milk (480 ml)

2 tbsp. of milk chocolate shavings

Preparation:

1. Dissolve the cacao powder and sugar together in the hot water, and continue to cook on a medium heat until the mixture begins to boil.
2. Add the milk until the beverage begins to boil.
3. Lower the flame and continue to stir on a low heat. Cook for approximately 5 minutes.
4. Pour into 2 large mugs
5. Shave 2 tbsp. of milk chocolate and add half of the shavings to each mugs.
6. Enjoy!

Variation...for adults:

After pouring the beverage into the mugs, add 5 ml of brandy to each glass and stir.

The first recipe in this book is a chocolate beverage that my mother used to make us as children, especially on winter days when the rain would beat down on our roof and windows.
My mother would cook cacao with sugar and milk. Now, as I write about this beverage, I imagine her stirring this aromatic and delicious drink, and then pouring a glass for my brother and I, topping it off with chocolate shavings... just the thought of it makes my mouth water!

PEANUT BUTTER CANDY

Ingredients for 20 oz (550 grams) of Candy:

1¾ oz (50 grams) of dark chocolate (chopped or in coins)

1¾ oz (50 grams) milk chocolate (chopped or in coins)

I cup of peanut butter

7 oz (200 grams) of powdered sugar

Preparation:

1. Cover a small square pan with a sheet of baking paper or prepare a silicon mold pan.
2. Melt the dark chocolate and the milk chocolate (chopped or in coins) in the microwave or in a double bottom pot.
3. Add the peanut butter and powdered sugar and stir into a smooth mixture.
4. Pour the mixture into the pan you prepared and stabilize it in the refrigerator.
5. If using a square pan, slice the candies into your desired size. Alternatively, release the candies from the mold pan.
6. Store the candies in a sealed container in the refrigerator.

CHOCOLATE SANDWICH SPREAD

Ingredients:

3 tbsp. of cacao

5 tbsp. of sugar

2 tbsp. of warm water for melting

5½ oz (150 grams) of butter

5 ml of vanilla extract

Preparation:

1. Mix the sugar, cacao and hot water.
2. Place the mixture on a medium heat and boil while stirring.
3. Reduce the heat and continue to cook for another 3 minutes, while stirring.
4. Turn off the heat.
5. Add the butter to the mixture and stir until it has melted.
6. Add 1 tsp. of vanilla extract and stir well.
7. Stir while cooling until the mixture becomes creamy.
8. Chill and transfer the mixture to a sealed container for storage.
9. Store in the refrigerator.

When I was in school, every day the kids would eat a sandwich with chocolate spread for their morning snack...usually whatever chocolate spread was sold at the nearest supermarket.

My mother, however, would make us her own special chocolate spread, one that she claims was healthier, with no preservatives or margarine.

SOFT CHOCOLATE CANDY

Ingredients for 3½ oz (100 grams) of candy:

3½ oz (100 grams) of quality dark chocolate, chopped or in coins

2 tbsp. of coconut oil

Preparation:

1. Melt the chocolate in the microwave – operate for 30 seconds, mix the chocolate, and continue to operate until it is fully melted.
2. Add the coconut oil and mix well.
3. Pour into paper cupcake molds and place in the refrigerator to stabilize for approximately 3 hours.
4. Store the candies in a sealed container at room temperature.

Variation:

Creamy milk or white chocolate candy

Replace the dark chocolate with milk or white chocolate and reduce the amount of coconut oil to one tbsp.

CHOCOLATE TAHINI CANDIES

Ingredients for 28 oz (800 grams) of candy:

1 cup of Raw Tahini

14 oz (400 grams) of chopped dark chocolate

3½ oz (100 grams) of Powdered Sugar

1¾ oz (50 grams) of sesame seeds

Preparation:

1. Line a small square pan or English cake pan with a sheet of baking paper or prepare as silicon mold pan with shapes and sizes of your choice.
2. Melt the chopped dark chocolate or dark chocolate coins in the microwave.
3. Mix the tahini with chocolate in a bowl until you reach a smooth mixture.
4. Add the powdered sugar and sesame seeds and stir well.
5. Transfer the mixture into the silicon molds or onto the pan and smooth it out. Place in the refrigerator for a few hours to stabilize.
6. If using a square pan, slice into squares of your desired size. Alternatively, remove the candies from the silicon mold pan.
7. Store the candies in a sealed container in the refrigerator.

CHOCOLATE FUDGE

Ingredients for 28 oz (800 grams) of fudge:

1 container (250 ml) of heavy whipping cream, 38% fat
2 cups of sugar (14 oz; 400 grams)
¼ cup of glucose (3 oz; 80 grams)
A pinch of salt
7 oz (200 grams) of dark chocolate, chopped or in coins
1 tsp vanilla extract

Preparation:

1. Line a small square pan or an English cake pan with baking paper or prepare a silicon mold pan in the shape and size of your choice.
2. Place the heavy whipping cream, sugar, glucose, salt and chocolate in a double-bottom pot and mix with a wooden spoon.
3. Very Important: Prior to boiling, if any sugar accumulates on the sides of the pot, lower all of the grains into the mixture using a wet pastry brush. From this moment onward, do not continue to stir!
4. Bring the mixture to a boil over medium heat and continue to cook (remember, do not stir!) until you reach a temperature of 114°C (237.2°F) (measure using a sugar thermometer).
5. Remove the pot from the stove and cool. When the mixture reaches the temperature of 46°C add the vanilla extract and stir with a clean dry wooden spoon until the mixture is firm and not shiny. This can take at least 10 minutes.
6. Pour the mixture into the baking pan and leave in room temperature for 10 hours for stabilizing.
7. Slice the fudge into cubes of the desired size.
8. Store the fudge in a closed container at room temperature.
9. Note: sometimes the fudge becomes too soft after it remains in the container. Allow to sit in fresh air for a few hours before serving and it will solidify.

Variation:

After Step 5, add 3½ oz (100 grams) of chopped roasted nuts or dried fruit. Continue according to the recipe.

EASY CHOCOLATE FUDGE

Ingredients for 28 oz (800 grams) of fudge:

1 can of sweetened condensed milk (14 oz; 400grams)

14 oz (400 grams) of 70% cacao dark chocolate, chopped or in coins

1¾ oz (50 grams) of chopped nuts / dried fruit (optional)

Preparation:

1. Line a small square pan with a sheet of baking paper.
2. Boil the sweetened condensed milk in the microwave, add the chocolate and mix well until it is melted.
   Optional: add the nuts or dried fruit and mix.
3. Pour the mixture into the pan and cool at room temperature.
4. Cut the cooled mixture into squares and store in a sealed container in the refrigerator.

Variation:

White Chocolate Easy Fudge Candies

Replace the dark chocolate with 21 oz (600 grams) of white chocolate.

Milk Chocolate Easy Fudge Candies

Replace the dark chocolate with 18 oz (500 grams) of milk chocolate.

CHOCOLATE COCONUT CANDY

Ingredients:

7 oz (200 grams) of coconut + 1¾ oz (50 grams) for the coating

14 oz (400 grams) of sweetened condensed milk

5½ oz (150 grams) of dark chocolate

Preparation:

1. Heat the sweetened condensed milk in the microwave for one minute.
2. Add the chocolate and stir.
3. Heat the mixture in the microwave for an additional 30 seconds. Stir until the chocolate melts. If needed, heat in the microwave for an additional 30 seconds.
4. Add the coconut and stir well.
5. Line a pan with a sheet of baking paper and line the sheet with half of the amount of coconut intended for coating.
6. Spread the mixture evenly on the pan lined with the coconut.
7. Sprinkle the remaining coconut flakes on top.
8. Stabilize in the refrigerator and cut into squares.

CHOCOLATE POPCORN

Ingredients:

3½ oz (100 grams) of prepared lightly salted popcorn

7 oz (200 grams) of sweetened condensed milk

5½ oz (150 grams) of dark chocolate

Preparation:

1. Boil the sweetened condensed milk in the microwave for one minute.
2. Add the chocolate and stir.
3. Spread out the popcorn on a baking pan.
4. Pour the chocolate mixture over the popcorn and mix using 2 forks.
5. Heat the chocolate covered popcorn in the oven for 15 minutes at 150°C (302°F), stirring once or twice while it is baking.
6. Let cool and enjoy!

CRUNCHY CHOCOLATE WITH ALMONDS

For this candy, it will be necessary to temper the chocolate (see on page 11)

This rich candy, once you begin to snack on crunchy chocolate, you won't stop!

Ingredients for 25 oz (700 grams) of candies:

17½ oz (500 grams) of milk chocolate, chopped or in coins
3½ oz (100 grams) of chopped almonds
½ cup sugar (3½ oz; 100 gr)
2 tbsp. of water (30 ml)

Preparation:

1. Place the water and sugar in a double bottom pot and stir with a wooden spoon on a medium heat until the sugar has melted.
2. Bring the syrup to a boil, add the almonds and continue to cook while constantly stirring with a wooden spoon until all the water has evaporated.
Important! Do not allow the sugar to turn into caramel in the pot!
3. Turn off the heat and continue to stir and then let cool.
4. Melt about ⅔ of the chocolate in the microwave – operate for 30 seconds, mix the chocolate, and continue to operate until it is fully melted.
5. Add the remaining chocolate and blend into a smooth mixture.
6. Add the sugar-coated almonds and stir.
7. Pour the mixture into an elongated pan and place in the refrigerator to stabilize.
8. Cut the candy and store in a sealed container at room temperature.

Extra sugar left in the pot of the almonds?
Use it to sweeten tea or add it to your cake recipe.

CHOCOLATE DISKS

For this candy, it will be necessary to temper the chocolate (see on page 11)

A spectacular candy that is easy to make. It can be made of dark, milk or white chocolate. I like to add roasted nuts and dried fruit to the dark chocolate (which slightly sweeten the bitterness of the chocolate).

It is best to add roasted and salted nuts to the milk chocolate (which balance out the sweetness of the chocolate) and to the white chocolate, I add roasted nuts.

Ingredients for approximately 20 pieces:

10 oz (300 grams) of dark, milk or white Chocolate – chopped or coin-shaped

3½ oz (100 grams) of your choice of nuts and/or dried fruit (refer to the forward of the recipe)

Preparation:

1. Lay out a silicon surface or a sheet of baking paper on the work surface.
2. Melt approximately ⅔ of the chocolate in the microwave for 30 seconds, then stir.
3. Continue to do so until the chocolate has fully melted. Add the rest of the chocolate and stir until you have a smooth mixture.
4. With the help of a spoon, pour the chocolate into circles on the silicon surface or baking paper and spread the nuts or dried fruit on top of them.
5. Let stabilize in room temperature.
6. Store the disks in a sealed container in room temperature.

CORNFLAKES CANDY

Ingredients for approximately 40 candies:

10 oz (300 grams) of milk chocolate, chopped or in coins

3½ oz (100 grams) of butter at room temperature

3½ oz (100 grams) of Cornflakes

Paper cupcake molds

Preparation:

1. Melt the chocolate in the microwave – heat for 30 seconds, stir, and continue in this manner until chocolate is fully melted.
2. Add the butter and stir together into a smooth mixture.
3. Add the Cornflakes and stir well.
4. Place a heaping tablespoon of the mixture into each cupcake mold.
5. Place in the refrigerator to stabilize.
6. Store the candies in a closed container in the refrigerator.

My mother was a pharmacist, and at this pharmacy, she wouldn't just concoct syrups and medicines, but recipes were shared between the employees and the customers and tastings were held. One day, my mother came home from work with a recipe for a candy that was made of equal parts chocolate, butter and cornflakes.

Throughout my entire childhood, we prepared this recipe at home. I upgraded it in recent years, so that it would be more of a candy and less of a cookie.

CHOCOLATE LOLLIPOP

For this candy, it will be necessary to temper the chocolate (see on page 11)

Chocolate lollipops are a favorite among children and they are easy to prepare. I did not specify the quantities of each ingredient. Use as much chocolate as you have available to you or as you wish. The size of the lollipop is also up to you!

Ingredients:

Chocolate of your desired flavor, chopped or in coins

Sprinkles or small candies for decoration

Special Equipment:

Lollipop sticks

Preparation:

1. Spread a silicon surface or a sheet of baking paper on your work surface.
2. Melt about ⅔ of the chocolate in the microwave – operate for 30 seconds, mix the chocolate, and continue to operate until it is fully melted.
3. Add the remaining chocolate and blend into a smooth mixture.
4. Pour the chocolate into circles onto the silicon or paper surface using a spoon, place a stick at the center of chocolate circle and turn the stick so that it will be covered by the melted chocolate on all sides.
5. Decorate the candy with the sprinkles and let stabilize at room temperature.
6. Store the candies in a sealed container at room temperature.

CHOCOLATE NUT LAYERS

Ingredients for 16 oz (450 grams) of layered candy:

For the first layer:
7 oz (200 grams) of dark chocolate, chopped or in coins

2 tbsp. of hazelnut spread (may be purchased at a specialty store)

1¾ oz (50 grams) of butter at room temperature

For the second layer:
5 oz (150 grams) of milk chocolate, chopped or in coins

3 tbsp. of hazelnut spread

1¾ oz (50 grams) of hazelnut bresilienne (may be purchased at a specialty store)

Preparation:

Preparing the first layer:
1. Melt the chocolate in the microwave – heat for 30 seconds, stir and continue in the same manner until chocolate is fully melted.
2. Add the butter and hazelnut spread to the melted chocolate and stir well.
3. Spread out the mixture in a medium square pan (a layer about ½ cm high) and place in the refrigerator to stabilize for 30 minutes.

Preparing the second layer:
1. Melt the milk chocolate in the microwave.
2. Add the hazelnut spread to the melted chocolate and stir well.
3. Sprinkle the hazelnut bresilienne on the first layer after it has stabilized, spread the second layer, and place back in the refrigerator for stabilization.
4. Slice the layers into strips or squares with a sharp knife.
5. Store the candies in a closed container in the refrigerator.

CHOCOLATE & SEED CANDY

For this candy, it will be necessary to temper the chocolate (see on page 11)

Ingredients for 5 oz (150 grams) of candy:

3 spoons sugar

3 spoons pumpkin seeds

5 oz (150 grams) of quality dark chocolate, chopped or in coins

Preparation:

1. Grease one small sheet of baking paper with the oil spray. Cover it with another small sheet so that the paper on top will be greased on its underside, and separate the papers. Prepare a rolling pin as well.
2. Toast the pumpkin seeds for a few minutes on an ungreased pan.
3. Place the sugar in a double bottom pot and heat over a medium heat. Stir gently with a wooden spoon until all the sugar dissolves, begins to boil and obtains a caramel color. Note: since this is a dry caramel, without the addition of water, make sure to watch that the sugar will not burn.
4. Turn off the heat, add seeds and stir well.
5. Flatten the mixture over one of the greased baking sheets and cover with the other sheet. Flatten with the rolling pin to create a very thin surface. and let cool.
6. Pound the surface you obtained with a rolling pin until you reach a course mixture.
7. Melt about ⅔ of the chocolate in the microwave – operate for 30 seconds, mix the chocolate, and continue to operate until it is fully melted.
8. Add the remaining chocolate and blend into a smooth mixture.
9. Add the ground seed candy to the melted chocolate and mix well.
10. Spread the mixture on a silicon surface or on a sheet of baking paper. Alternatively, pour the mixture into a shallow mold pan.
11. Place in the refrigerator to stabilize.
12. Break the candy into uneven pieces using your hands or remove the candies from the mold pan.
13. Store the candies in a sealed container at room temperature.

{ 2 }

TRUFFLES

Truffles are my favorite kind of chocolate – they are so creamy and just melt in my mouth. They can be coated in cacao, in sugar, or in chocolate.

Truffles are easy to make and can be enjoyed on many different occasions. They are often served for special events such as weddings or showers, or given as gifts...but I can't help but snack on them whenever they are around!

CHOCOLATE TRUFFLES BASIC RECIPE

Ingredients for approximately 70 truffles:

17½ oz (500 grams) of quality dark chocolate or

23 oz (650 grams) of milk chocolate, chopped or in coins

1 container (250 ml) of heavy whipping cream, 38% fat

1 tbsp. of glucose

1¾ oz (50 grams) of softened butter

1 tsp of flavored extract such as vanilla, almond, orange, lemon, raspberry or mint

For the coating:

3½ oz (100 grams) of cacao powder or 150 grams of powdered sugar

Preparation:

1. Place the chocolate in a bowl.
2. Heat the heavy whipping cream and glucose in a pot to a boil. Once mixture has boiled, remove it from the stove.
3. Pour the heavy whipping cream on the chocolate, add the butter and stir until a smooth mixture is achieved.
4. Add your desired flavor extract and stir.
5. Cool at room temperature and then cover the bowl and place in the refrigerator to stabilize for at least 3 hours.
6. Roll the mixture into balls and dip into either the cacao powder or the powdered sugar (the powdered sugar hardens after one to two days and creates a hard coating).
7. Store the truffles in a sealed container in the refrigerator.

Variation:

White Chocolate Truffles

Use 26 oz (750 grams) of chocolate and do not use butter.

Citrus-Scented Truffles

If selecting a lemon or orange flavor extract, you may combine shredded lemon or orange peels into the cacao for the coating, which enriches the fruity scent.

Chocolate Almond Truffles

If selecting an almond or amaretto flavor extract, you may roll the truffles in ground almonds.

TRUFFLES WITH ALCOHOL

Ingredients for approximately 70 truffles:

21 oz (600 grams) of quality dark chocolate, chopped or in coins

1 container (250 ml) of heavy whipping cream, 38% fat

1 tbsp. of glucose

1¾ oz (50 grams) of butter

2 tbsp. of brandy or liqueur

For the Coating:

7 oz (200 grams) of quality dark chocolate, chopped or in coins

1¾ oz (50 grams) of cacao powder

Preparation:

1. Place the chocolate in a bowl.
2. Bring the heavy whipping cream and the glucose to a boil. Once boiling, immediately remove from stove.
3. Pour the heavy whipping cream on the chocolate, add the butter and mix everything well into an even mixture.
4. Add the alcohol and mix.
5. Cool at room temperature and afterwards, cover the bowl and place in the refrigerator to stabilize for at least 3 hours.
6. Melt in the microwave the chocolate for the coating.
7. Roll the mixture into balls, dip them in the melted chocolate and then in the cacao powder.
8. Store the truffles in a sealed container in the refrigerator.

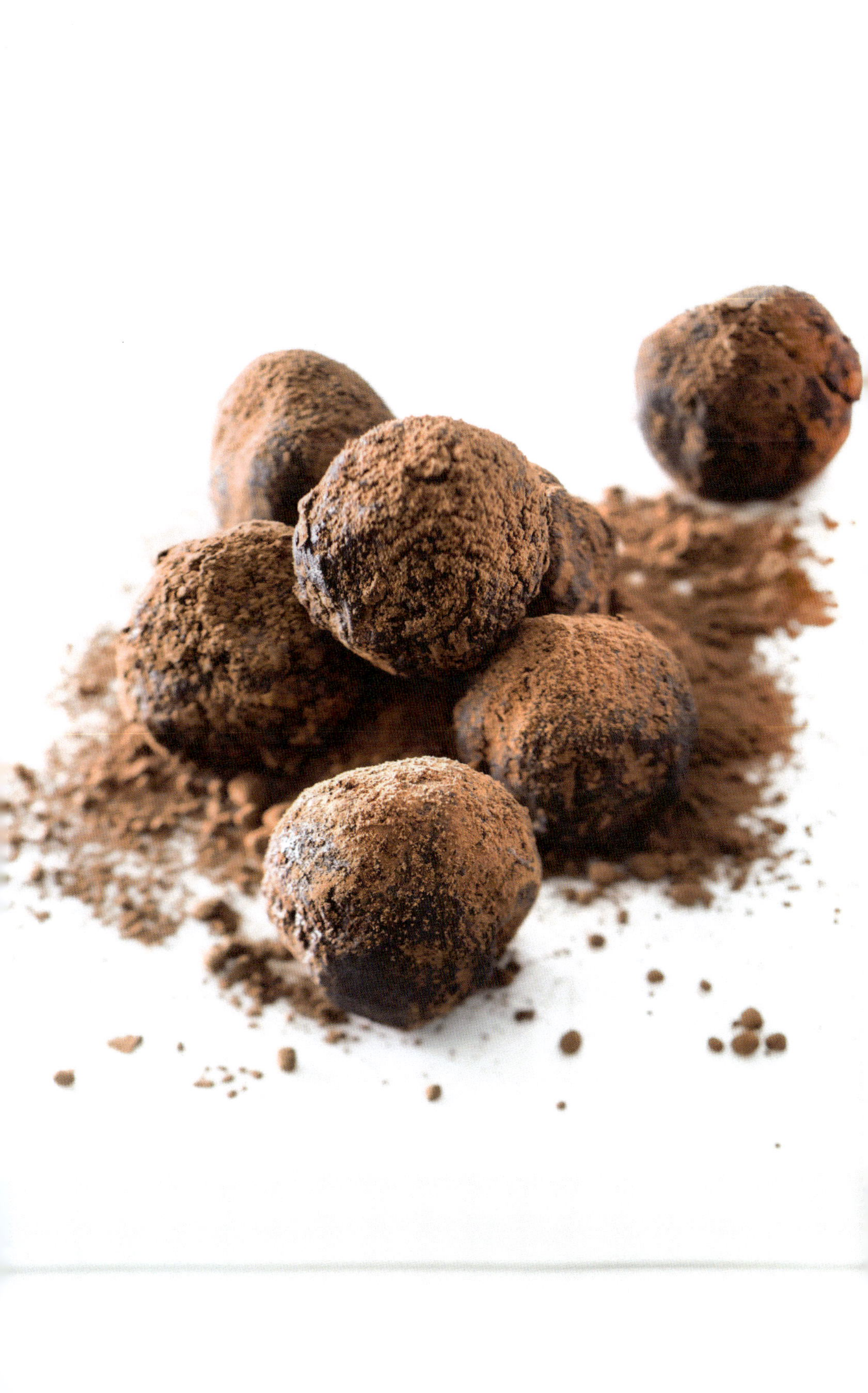

COCONUT TRUFFLES

Ingredients for approximately 45 Truffles:

½ container (200 ml) of coconut cream

10 oz (300 grams) of milk chocolate, chopped or in coins

3½ oz (100 grams) of quality dark chocolate, chopped or in coins

1¾ oz (50 grams) of coconut flakes

For the Coating:

1¾ oz (50 grams) grams of coconut flakes

Preparation:

1. Bring the coconut cream to a boil in the microwave.
2. Add the two types of chocolates and mix well. Add the coconut and mix again.
3. Cool the mixture at room temperature and afterwards, cover the bowl and place in the refrigerator to stabilize for at least 3 hours.
4. Roll the mixture into balls and dip in the coconut flakes.
5. Store the truffles in a sealed container in the refrigerator.

NUT TRUFFLES

Ingredients for approximately 70 truffles:

17½ oz (500 grams) of quality dark chocolate or

23 oz (650 grams) of

milk chocolate, chopped or in coins

1 container (250 ml) or heavy whipping cream, 38% fat

1 tbsp. of glucose

3 tbsp. of pistachio spread, hazelnut spread or almond spread (can be found in a specialty store)

For the Coating:

3½ oz (100 grams) of hazelnut bresilienne (can be found in a specialty store) or ground pistachios or almonds

Preparation:

1. Place the chocolate in a bowl.
2. Heat the heavy whipping cream and glucose in a pot to a boil. Once mixture has boiled, remove it from the stove.
3. Pour the heavy whipping cream on the chocolate and stir until a smooth mixture is achieved.
4. Add the pistachio / hazelnut / almond spread and stir well.
5. Cool at room temperature and then cover the bowl and place in the refrigerator to stabilize for at least 3 hours.
6. Roll the mixture into balls and dip into one of the coatings – based on the chosen spread.
7. Store the truffles in a sealed container in the refrigerator.

FRUIT TRUFFLES

Ingredients for approximately 20 truffles:

7 oz (200 grams) of the chocolate of your choice – dark, milk or white – chopped or in coins

1¾ oz (50 grams) of natural fruit puree or frozen fruit puree (can be purchased at a specialty store)

1 tbsp. of glucose

For the Coating:

3½ oz (100 grams) of powdered sugar, cacao powder or small chocolate sprinkles

Preparation:

1. Place the fruit puree and glucose in a sauce pan and bring to a boil on low heat, while stirring with a whisk.
2. Add the chocolate, reduce the heat as low as possible and continue to cook while mixing with a whisk until the chocolate will melt and assimilate into the mixture.
3. Cool the mixture at room temperature and afterwards, cover the bowl and place in the refrigerator to stabilize for at least 3 hours.
4. Roll the mixture into balls. Optional: roll the balls in the powdered sugar (which hardens after one or two days and creates a hard coating) or in the cacao powder or chocolate sprinkles.
5. Store the truffles in a closed container in the refrigerator.

A customer requested that I prepare for her husband chocolate candies with fruit. After a few attempts, I was able to create fruity chocolate candies, surprising in their taste.

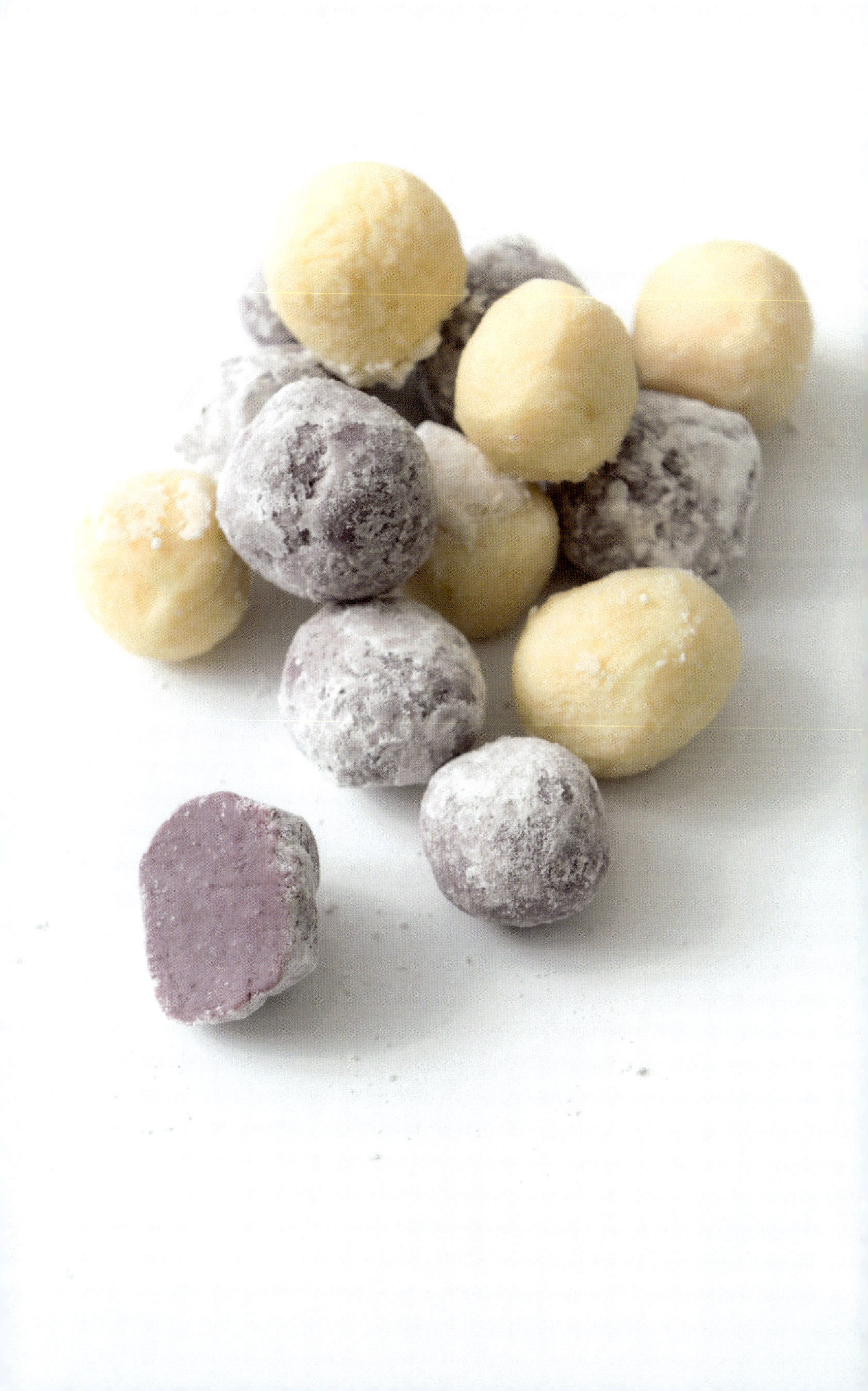

{ 3 }

CHOCOLATE CANDIES WITH FILLING

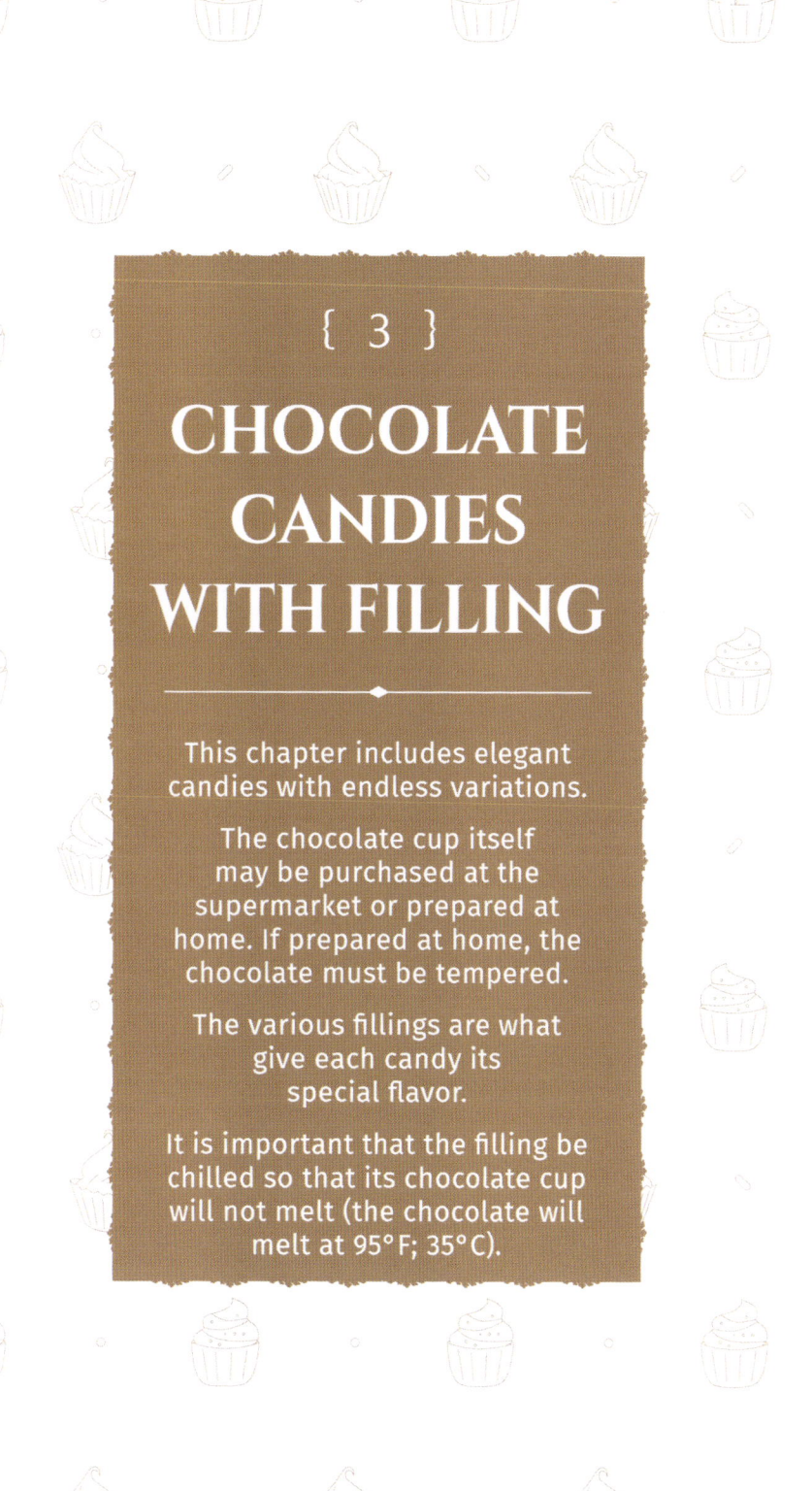

This chapter includes elegant candies with endless variations.

The chocolate cup itself may be purchased at the supermarket or prepared at home. If prepared at home, the chocolate must be tempered.

The various fillings are what give each candy its special flavor.

It is important that the filling be chilled so that its chocolate cup will not melt (the chocolate will melt at 95°F; 35°C).

HOMEMADE CHOCOLATE CUPS

Note: To make the chocolate cups, you must temper the chocolate first (see instructions on page 11).

Preparation:

Chocolate cups may be prepared in one of two ways:

Method 1:

1. Pour 1 tsp. of tempered chocolate into each extra small paper cupcake mold.
2. Using the back of the spoon, spread the chocolate from the base of the cup to the walls of the paper cupcake mold.
3. Stabilize the cups at room temperature or in the freezer for 10 minutes.
4. Peel the paper cupcake molds from the chocolate so you are left with a small chocolate cup.

Method 2:

1. Pour the tempered chocolate into cup-shaped molds for chocolate (can be plastic, silicon, polycarbonate, etc.) until each mold is filled with chocolate.
2. Hit the mold pan against the work surface to remove all air bubbles.
3. Flip the mold pan filled with chocolate upside-down until the chocolate will begin to rain down into a large bowl below.
4. Using a spatula, remove excess chocolate from the pan into the bowl.
5. Stabilize the remaining chocolate in the upside-down pan at room temperature or in the freezer for 10 minutes (pan must remain upside-down during this time).
6. After stabilizing, remove the chocolate cups from the mold pan.

BASIC CHOCOLATE GANACHE

Ingredients for 40-50 prepared chocolate cups:

12½ oz (350 grams) of quality dark chocolate or 16 oz (450 grams) of milk chocolate or 17½ oz (500 grams) of white chocolate, chopped or in coins

1 container (250 ml) of heavy whipping cream, 38% fat

For a flavor addition:

One tsp. of flavor extract such as vanilla, almond, orange, lemon, raspberry or mint

OR

2 tbsp. or brandy or liqueur of your choice

For garnish:

Chocolate sprinkles, rainbow sprinkles, chocolate flakes, etc.

Preparation:

1. Place the chocolate in a bowl.
2. Bring the heavy whipping cream to a boil in a sauce pan. Once boiled, immediately turn off the heat.
3. Pour the boiling whipping cream over the chocolate and mix into a smooth mixture.
4. Add the flavor extract or alcohol and mix. Optional: divide the mixture into a few small bowls and add a different flavor extract or alcohol to each one.
5. Cool the ganache completely at room temperature and pour into the chocolate cups.
6. This is the time to garnish the filled chocolate cups as you wish.
7. Store the filled chocolate cups in a sealed container in the refrigerator.

Variation:

Cool the ganache in the refrigerator (for about 2 hours) and whip – this makes the ganache lighter and airier. Place the ganache in a pastry bag with a decorating tip and squeeze into the chocolate cups.

WHITE CHOCOLATE GANACHE & FRUIT FILLING

Ingredients for approximately 50 cups of prepared chocolate cups:

17½ oz (500 grams) of white chocolate, chopped or in coins

1 container (250 ml) of heavy whipping cream, 38% fat

2 tbsp. of concentrated fruit puree in a flavor of your choice (may be purchased at a specialty store)

Preparation:

1. Place the chocolate in a bowl.
2. Bring the heavy whipping cream to a boil in a sauce pan. Once boiling, turn off heat immediately.
3. Pour the boiling whipping cream over the chocolate and mix well.
4. Melt the fruit puree in the microwave, add to the ganache and mix well.
5. Cool the ganache at room temperature and afterwards, cover and place in the refrigerator for at least 2 hours.
6. Whip the cold ganache, place in a pastry bag and squeeze into the chocolate cups.
7. Store the filled cups in a sealed container in the refrigerator.

HAZELNUT OR PISTACHIO FILLING

Ingredients for approximately 40-50 prepared chocolate cups:

17½ oz (500 grams) of white chocolate, chopped or in coins

1 container (250 ml) of heavy whipping cream, 38% fat

2 tbsp. of hazelnut spread

1¾ oz (50 grams) of hazelnut bresilienne (can be purchased at a specialty store)

For decoration:

1¾ oz (50 grams) of hazelnut bresilienne

Preparation:

1. Place the chocolate in a bowl.
2. Bring the heavy whipping cream to a boil in a sauce pan. Once boiled, immediately turn off the heat.
3. Pour the boiling heavy whipping cream on the chocolate and mix well.
4. Add the hazelnut spread to the ganache and mix well. Add the hazelnut bresilienne as well and mix.
5. Cool the filling at room temperature and afterwards, cover and place in the refrigerator for at least 2 hours.
6. Fill the chocolate cups with the filling and decorate with the hazelnut bresilienne.
7. Store the filled chocolate cups in a sealed container in the refrigerator.

Variation:

Replace the white chocolate with 400 grams of milk chocolate. Replace the hazelnut spread with pistachio spread and the hazelnut bresilienne – both in the mixture and decoration – with finely chopped pistachios.

CHEESE FILLING

Ingredients for approximately 25-30 prepared chocolate cups:

3½ oz (100 grams) of cream cheese

7 oz (200 grams) of powdered sugar

1 tsp. of flavor extract such as vanilla, lemon, strawberry, raspberry, blackberry or mint

A few drops of food coloring

Preparation:

1. Place the cream cheese and powdered sugar in an electric mixer bowl with a flat beater and mix into an even mixture.
2. Add the flavor extract and food coloring and mix until they are assimilated into the cheese.
3. Fill the chocolate cups with the whipped cheese filling.
4. Store the filled chocolate cups in a sealed container in the refrigerator.

PINA COLADA FILLING

Ingredients for approximately 50 prepared chocolate cups:

14 oz (400 grams) of white chocolate, chopped or in coins

200 ml of coconut cream

2 tbsp. of Pina colada liqueur

For the Coating:

1¾ oz (50 grams) of dark or milk chocolate, chopped or in coins

1¾ oz (50 grams) of coconut flakes

Preparation:

1. Place the chocolate in a bowl.
2. Bring the coconut cream to a boil in the microwave.
3. Pour the boiling cream over the chocolate and mix well.
4. Add the Pina colada liqueur to the ganache and mix well.
5. Cool the filling at room temperature and afterwards, cover it and place in the refrigerator to stabilize for an hour.
6. Fill the chocolate cups.
7. Melt the chocolate for the coating in the microwave and pour over the filling. Sprinkle some coconut flakes over the chocolate.
8. Store the filled chocolate cups in a sealed container in the refrigerator.

MARSHMALLOW CREAM FILLING

Ingredients for approximately 40 prepared chocolate cups:

½ tbsp. of gelatin

½ cup cold water

½ cup water (at room temperature)

2 cups sugar

½ cup glucose

A pinch of salt

1 tsp of vanilla extract

1 tbsp. boiling water

For the Coating:

1¾ oz (50 grams) of dark or milk chocolate, chopped or in coins

Preparation:

1. Place gelatin and cold water in a small bowl and gently stir. Set aside.
2. Place water, sugar, glucose and salt in a double bottom pot and stir gently with a wooden spoon.
3. **Very Important:** Prior to boiling, if any sugar accumulates on the sides of the pot, lower all of the grains into the mixture using a wet pastry brush. From this moment onward, **do not continue to stir!**
4. Bring the mixture to a boil over a medium heat and continue to cook (remember, do not stir!) until you reach a temperature of 124°C (255.2°F) (measure using a sugar thermometer). Turn off the heat.

Preparing the marshmallow cream mixture:

1. Place the bowl with the gelatin in the microwave for 20-25 seconds to dissolve.
2. Pour the boiling syrup and melted gelatin into a mixing bowl. Whip for 2 minutes on low speed (watch out – the liquid is boiling!) and ten more minutes on high speed.
3. Lower the whipping speed, add 1 tsp of vanilla extract and boiling water and whip for a minute until absorbed in the mixture.
4. Cool the marshmallow cream completely until it reaches room temperature.
5. Fill the chocolate cups using a wet spoon.
6. Melt the chocolate for the coating in the microwave and pour over the filling.
7. Wait at least 6 hours for stabilizing.
8. Store the filled chocolate cups in a sealed container at room temperature.

TOFFEE FILLING

Ingredients for approximately 35-40 prepared chocolate cups:

1 container (250 ml) of heavy whipping cream, 38% fat

1 cup of white sugar

½ cup of brown sugar

3½ oz (100 grams) of butter

½ cup of glucose

A pinch of salt

½ tsp. of vanilla extract

For the Garnish:

Nuts, melted chocolate or chocolate flakes

Preparation:

1. Place the heavy whipping cream, the two types of sugar, butter, glucose and salt in a double-bottom pot and mix with a wooden spoon.
2. **Very Important:** Prior to boiling, if any sugar accumulates on the sides of the pot, lower all of the grains into the mixture using a wet pastry brush. From this moment onward, **do not continue to stir!**
3. Bring the mixture to a boil over medium heat and continue to cook (remember, do not stir!) until you reach a temperature of 114°C (237.2°F) (measure using a sugar thermometer).
4. Remove the pot from the burner, immediately add the vanilla extract and mix with a clean and dry wooden spoon until the extracts assimilates into the syrup. Cool completely at room temperature.
5. Fill the chocolate cups and garnish with the decoration of your choice.
6. Store the filled chocolate cups in a sealed container at room temperature.

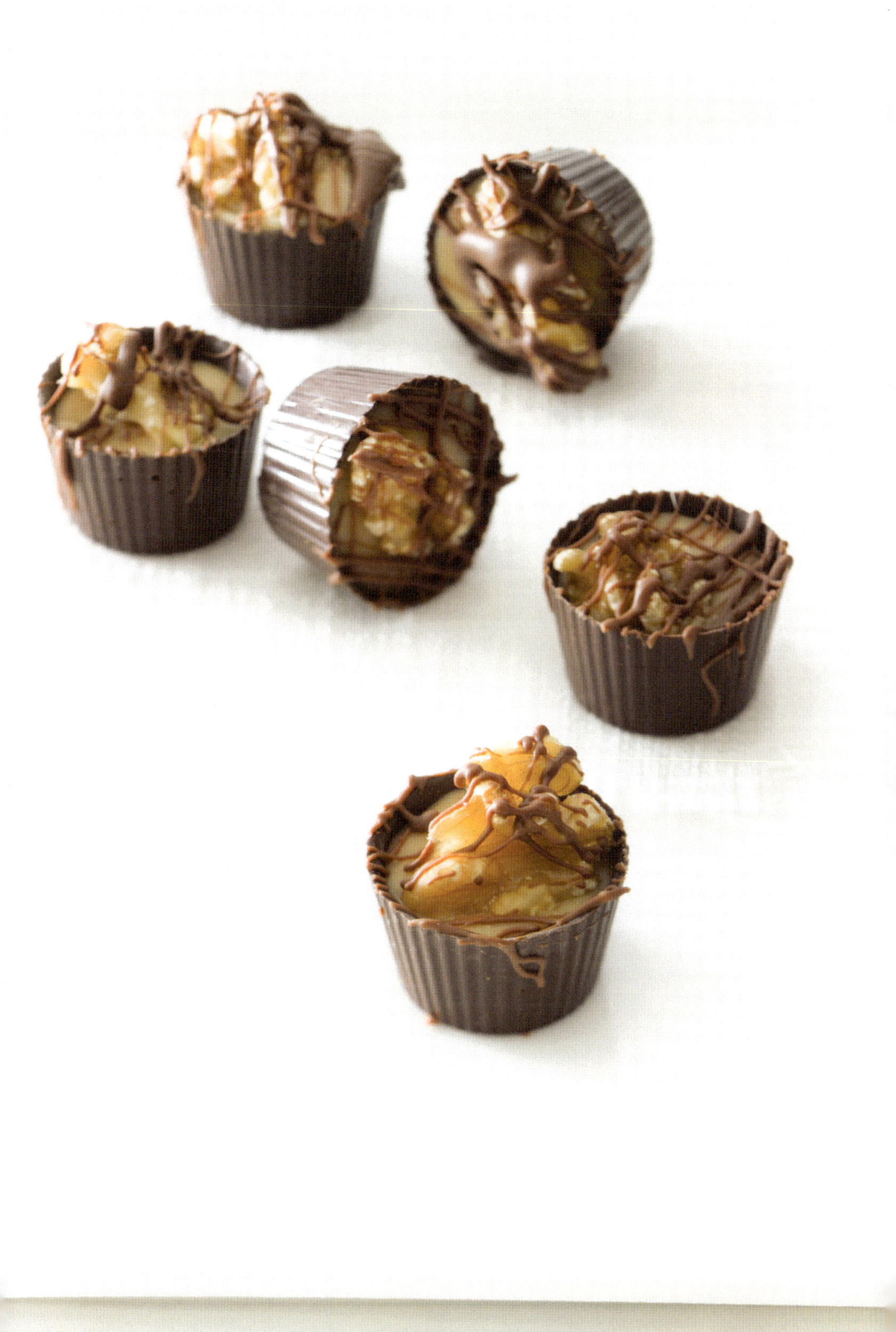

Printed in Great Britain
by Amazon